Kill It with Social Media

How eBay, Amazon, & Etsy Sellers Are Exploding Their
Business with Facebook, Twitter, & Pinterest

Table of Contents

Social Media Marketing for eBay Sellers

Do you really need to blow up social media to sell on eBay and Amazon?

It's sort of like asking, are you a glass is half full, or a glass is half empty type of person. If you're a glass is half full type, you're going to scream "Damn right! You have to be on social media, because—that's where the people are." If you're a glass is half empty type you're going to whine and moan "what's the point? I'm selling my stuff on eBay, not on Facebook and Twitter."

You probably see where I'm going with this.

Online sellers are divided on the need for social media, its uses, and its outcomes. Some sellers will tell you they couldn't have gotten where they are without it, others will say "Why bother!" or "Hey! I tried it, and it didn't make any diff. My sales stayed the same."

I'm going to try not to take sides here. My goal is to give you the information you need to implement social media in your eBay business should you choose to do so.

My primary focus is going to be on Facebook, Twitter, and Pinterest because they are the three powerhouses behind social media today. Facebook and Twitter get more of the space, because they are the social media sites everybody goes to. Pinterest gets a bigger mention because it is the one seller's say actually works best.

Does that mean you need to use all three? Or that you should focus exclusively on Pinterest because it's what works best for most sellers? No. It means you should start out slow. Pick one or two social media platforms and spend ten or fifteen minutes on them two or three days a week.

A PEW University study on social media usage has one more relevant piece of information for savvy online marketers— over half of the people who visit social media sites are active on more than one site. For marketers the implication is clear, if you want to reach your primary customer base, you need to be active on several social media platforms. Using one social media platform isn't going to cut it. Think a minimum of two, maybe even three social media platforms if you want to reach your target audience effectively.

When you are first getting started watch what other sellers in businesses similar to yours are doing on social media sites. Like some of their posts and start building your network. Make a few short posts. Put up a few pictures, or some short videos. Rinse and repeat.

The key to success with social media is to post regularly, comment when someone likes or comments on one of your posts, and keep a conversation going with your followers. Over time you will develop a following of your own.

And, one other tip, don't try to move too quickly, or fast track your way to success. There are a lot of places on and off of eBay where you can buy 500 or 1,000 likes. Don't be tempted. Phantom fans who don't comment on your posts, or like them, aren't going to do your business any good over the long haul.

Remember, it's not a contest to see who can get the most followers. It's all about getting the most followers who will engage with you on a regular basis, and who will share your content with their friends and followers.

That's how you build your business using social media. Give more than you get, share content your followers like, enjoy, and can use. If you do this, sales will follow.

. . . .

Before I go any further let me tell you a little more about me, so you can understand why I'm the right guy to help you grow your eBay business.

Why listen to me?

Hey there, Nick Vulich here.

If you're like me, I'm sure you're probably a little skeptical about taking advice from someone without knowing a little bit about them first.

I've been selling on eBay since 1999. Most of my online customers know me as history-bytes. I've also operated as its old news, back door video, and sports card one.

I've sold 30,004 items for a total of $411,755.44 over the past fifteen years, and that's just on my history-bytes id. I've cut way back on eBay selling over the past year so I can focus on my writing, but I still keep my hat in the game. That way I can keep current with the challenges my readers face every day when they go to sell on eBay.

I've been an eBay Power Seller or Top Rated Seller for most of the past fifteen years, which means I've met eBay's sales and customer satisfaction goals.

This is the tenth book I've written about selling on eBay. The first two, *Freaking Idiots Guide to Selling on eBay*, and *eBay Unleashed*, are aimed more towards how to get started selling on eBay. *eBay Subject Matter Expert* suggests a different approach to selling on eBay – building a platform where customers recognize you as an expert in your niche, and buy from you because of your knowledge in that field. *Sell It Online* gives a brief overview of selling on eBay, Amazon, Etsy, and Fiver. *How to Make Money*

Selling Old Books & Magazines on eBay talks specifically about what I know best, how to sell books and magazines on eBay.

eBay Bookkeeping Made Easy helps sellers understand how to keep track of the money they are making, and how to take advantage of the tax code to make even more money. *eBay Shipping Simplified* helps sellers determine the best way to ship their items, and how to use eBay's shipping tools to make the task easier.

eBay 2015 is my longest book to date, and encapsulates everything sellers need to know to start and grow their eBay business.

Nearly two-thirds of this book originally appeared in *eBay Business Expert*. This work includes sections on Google+ and LinkedIn. It also includes transcripts of interviews with several other eBay sellers to give you a hands-on look at how other sellers approach social media marketing as a tool to grow their eBay businesses.

Social Media by the Numbers

According to a PEW University study published in 2014 seventy-one percent of adults who use the internet are on Facebook. Twitter, LinkedIn, Instagram, and Pinterest lag way behind with adult usage rates that fall somewhere between 23 to 28 percent.

Here are a few key takeaways for anyone planning to use social media to grow their online business.

- 31 percent of seniors are on Facebook.
- 53 percent of young adults age 18 to 29 are on Instagram. And, over half of these users visit the site daily.
- Women are three times more likely to use Pinterest than men. 42 percent of women who use the internet are on Pinterest, versus 13 percent of men.

If you need more help in choosing the correct social media platform to reach your key demographics check out the rest of the PEW University study.

Facebook users are aging with a larger percentage of seniors over age sixty-five on the site. Women are more likely to frequent Facebook than men.

Twitter usage is higher among young adults ages eighteen to twenty-nine, and falls off sharply among users over age forty-nine. Young adults and Afro-Americans are more likely to engage on Twitter.

Instagram has a high usage rate among young Americans ages eighteen to twenty-nine, and among Afro-Americans.

Pinterest users are primarily women, who tend to be college educated and more affluent.

LinkedIn is used less than other social media sites, but could be helpful if you are marketing to individuals between the ages of fifty to sixty-five. LinkedIn users also tend to be college graduates, with a higher annual household income.

The PEW University study does leave out one important group—teenagers.

If you're marketing primarily to teens you need to check out a 2014 study by Piper Jaffray … Taking Stock With Teens – Fall 2014.

Here's some of the information you will discover.

- You're message better look good on an iPhone, because 67 percent of teenagers either have or plan on getting an iPhone.
- Instagram and Twitter is the social media site most frequented by teens. So if teens are your target audience you need to include more pictures, video, and music in your posts, and fewer words.

- Pinterest is the least used social media site among teens.
- Facebook is used by fifty percent of all teens, but is not as popular as it was in the past.

Before I go into specifics on the individual social media sites here's something you need to understand: the people you want to reach spend a large portion of their day online. Many of them rarely if ever leave social media sites, so if you don't engage with them there, you're not going to be able to sell to them— period.

Facebook

Facebook is the big kid on the block in social media marketing. It used to be the "in" site for kids, but now that it has gone main-stream Facebook has become the primary social media platform used by marketers to reach women, age thirty-five to sixty.

If you haven't checked your Facebook News Feed lately one of the first things you'll notice is the changes in the content you see. Many of the top posts shown in your News Feed today are paid spots Facebook considers relevant to your interests. Your friend's posts are still there, but they're intermixed with paid content Facebook thinks might grab your interest, and make them a few bucks to boot.

Something else you need to understand is the majority of Facebook users access the site only from mobile devices. This means you need to keep your posts short, with quick easy to load pictures and videos. You should also check out every post you make to ensure it looks good on an Android or IOS (Apple) device.

Getting started

Facebook is all about engaging with other users. That means your primary goal is to provide content that makes users want to like, comment on, and share your posts. Forget selling, instead think engagement.

How do you do that?

Look at the popular posts in your News Feed, the ones users have liked and shared. The odds are they have at least one thing in common. Nine times out of ten they are visually oriented, which means they contain pictures or videos.

Facebook pictures come in a number of varieties, but they all share one common trait. They're of a person, or a cute furry pet—maybe even a baby. They're of a person making a funny face, or stuck in a strange place, or doing something unusual. Other times it's a picture of someone famous along with one of their quotes.

Better to be silent and thought a fool than to speak out and remove all doubt

If you pay attention you will see dozens of similar pictures in your News Feed every week. Some of them are cartoon images with catchy phrases; others are quotes from famous people. Many are product images with tag lines that scream out – "new from" … "on sale now" … "check out our new line of."

These types of images are a great way to catch people's attention, and garner a bunch of quick likes and shares. The thing to remember when creating your own items like these is to keep it legal. Don't just grab pictures you like off of the internet and add a snazzy quote. Make sure the image is copyright free. If you're in doubt the best way to select a "legal" picture is to visit a clip art site and invest a few bucks to pay for one time rights to use the image. Two such sites I use all of the time are Dollar Photo Club and Can Stock Photo. Most of the images on these sites cost under five bucks, less if you buy multiple credits, and they're easy to manipulate using MS Paint so you can create awesome sharable images.

Videos are hot on social media, and if your video catches on it can go viral quickly and spread across the internet.

Make your videos tasteful and keep them focused on your product line. In my case I sell old books and magazine articles. One video I include in all of my eBay listings is of Professor Puppet explaining my business and the types of items I sell. It helps people understand what my business is all about.

Other videos that would complement my product line would be reviews of historical books, how to videos about book and magazine collecting, and special interest videos on historical events. Each of them would promote interest in the types of items I sell.

When I purchased my first Otterbox case I was totally stumped about how to get it apart. Sure it came with a short set of directions in a smattering of different languages, but that wasn't enough to help me install the case. To get my phone inside of my new Otterbox I had to search YouTube for a quick tutorial. (If you haven't discovered it, the trick to removing that thin outer shell is to slip a credit card underneath and pry it up. Thanks again, YouTube.)

Anyone who sells smartphones or accessories for them should have a similar video on their Facebook page, and in their eBay item listing. It's good customer service, and it's likely to be shared time and again bringing customers back to your eBay listing and Facebook page. *Tip: if you decide to include someone else's video or photo in your listings or on your blog or website—get permission first. Contrary to popular belief, most pictures and video on the internet are copyrighted so it is illegal to reproduce them without proper permission.*

If you sell men's, women's, or children's clothes every new season, or product line you take on gives you the opportunity to add a new video to your Facebook page. If you're unsure how to do this check out Lauren's Fab Finds for more ideas.

Create more effective Facebook posts

There's a boatload of advice available about how to create more effective Facebook posts. Here's a short list that should help you boost audience engagement.

1. Keep your words to a minimum. Social media is constantly evolving and the most effective posts are visually oriented. If you want to maintain user engagement keep any text short—80 to 120 characters should be the max.

2. Don't link to stuff off of Facebook. Facebook users prefer to stay in their own little world.

3. Don't over sell. Facebook users are leery of marketing, and are quick to steer away from sales pitches.

4. Don't post the same content on Facebook that you do on other social media sites. Your followers expect and deserve new and exciting content, not yesterday's news, or recycled post from Twitter or your blog. Don't disappoint them.

How to Sell on Facebook

All of this begs the question if people don't like to be sold to on Facebook, how do you get them to buy your stuff?

That's a good question and one smart seller's are working hard to crack. The key is to understand what brings people to social media sites in the first place.

According to an April 2013 study published in The Atlantic the number one and three reason people go on social media sites is voyeurism. Facebook is the perfect tool to spy on your neighbors and friends. The catch is: Facebook users are consensual Peeking Tom's. We give each other permission to poke their noses into our back doors.

The number two reason people say they visit social media sites is to relieve boredom. They've got nothing better to do, so they turn to Facebook, Twitter, and similar sites to live vicariously through others.

And, the final reason given for visiting social media sites is to message between friends.

So, there you have it.

1. Voyeurism
2. Boredom
3. Messaging

If you are using social media to reach these people you need to play to these needs.

Every post, picture, and video you place on social media sites needs to take people behind the scenes, and give them a sneak peek of what your business or industry is all about. Make it personal, make it entertaining, show vulnerability, and poke fun at yourself.

At the same time, you need to make sure your posts are engaging. Encourage communication with your social media followers, and schedule time every day to follow up with them. If someone comments on one of your posts, respond to them, even if it's just to say "thanks" or "hi."

If you do these things, your posts will play into the reasons people visit social media sites.

Basics of Facebook Marketing

Create a Facebook Fan Page. Don't use your personal Facebook page. It's unprofessional, and it doesn't give you all of the tools you need to engage with your followers.

It's easy to create a Facebook Fan Page. Go to https://www.facebook.com/pages/create.php.

That's going to bring up the following page where you select the category to place your Facebook Fan Page in.

The choices are:

1. Local Business or Place
2. Company, Organization or institution
3. Brand or Product
4. Artist, band, or Public Figure
5. Entertainment
6. Cause, or Community

Local Business or Place

Company, Organization or Institution

Brand or Product

Artist, Band or Public Figure

Entertainment

Cause or Community

Select the category that best describes your business. For most online sellers it's going to be local business or place, or brand or product, depending upon how you're trying to promote yourself. If you're an author, artist, or musician choose artist, band, or public figure. It's pretty self-explanatory.

The next step is to set up your Facebook page, and give it a name. Your page name should be a no-brainer. If you have a business name or eBay store name that should be the name of your Facebook page. Make it easy for buyers to find you.

Make sure to fill out the about section, and provide a link to your eBay store. Add appropriate keywords in the about section. In my case, I sell historical collectibles so I would want to work in several of the following keywords, "vintage historical collectibles—magazine articles, prints, and advertisements." This will make it easier for search engines to locate your page, and for viewers to learn what you're all about.

Another neat feature you will find at the top of your page is the ability to *create a call to action button.* This button gives you a number of different choices including—shop now, contact us, use app, watch video, book now, sign up, or play game. If you're an online seller I'd suggest using shop now and linking to your eBay store, and Sign up with a link to your email list sign up form. If you choose only one call to action make it the sign up form for your email list. It will give you the biggest bang for your buck over the long haul.

Create an amazing Timeline Cover Photo. This is the rectangular image at the top of your Facebook page. It needs to reach out and grab viewer's attention. It could be one large photo or a collage of smaller photos showing yourself, your employees, or the products you sell. It may also be a good idea to add a tagline or your business name to your Timeline Cover Photo.

Keep in mind it's one of the first things people see when they come to your Facebook page so you want to do your best to make it stand out, and grab people's attention. With that said, here's my best advice—don't do it yourself. Hire a designer on Fiverr or elance to put together a professional design for you.

You also need to create a profile photo. Some sellers use their logo; others use a photo of one of their better selling products. My suggestion is to use a selfie. Studies show people are more likely to engage with photos of people, so give them what they want. Flash a big smile. If your audience would enjoy a joke—stick your tongue out at them, or make a funny face. A lot of sellers get all fancied up and wear a suit or dress. That's okay, but my thought is you should present a more casual appearance.

Dress like you normally would. This will make it easier for people to connect with you.

Now it's time to start adding your first posts.

This is what scares a lot of people, but it's one of the easiest parts about creating a Facebook page if you give it some thought. Think about yourself for a moment. What type of content do you enjoy engaging with on Facebook? Chances are you said—videos, pictures, and short entertaining posts.

That's the type of content you need to give your fan page visitors.

Create a couple of short two to three minute videos that explain your business, and talk about the products you sell; introduce your employees; interview a few of your customers, and let them say what they like about doing business with you. Post a few pictures of products you sell. Put up a humorous photo of your dog or cat playing with your computer or crawling out of a packing box. Post a picture of a hot new product you're getting ready to list.

The truth is there are all sorts of things you can post about. You just need to place yourself in your buyer's shoes and figure out what they'd like to know about your business or product line.

eBay Store Apps

There are a number of apps that let you place your eBay store on your Facebook fan page. Some are more feature filled or work better than others, so I'm giving you a list of apps you can explore.

Auction Items Facebook App

https://apps.facebook.com/auctionitems/. This one lets you put your eBay store in a tab on your Facebook fan page. They also have apps available for Etsy and Bonanza store owners.

Easy Social Shop App

http://www.easysocialshop.com/ebay-facebook-shop/. This is another free and easy solution to get started selling on eBay.

StoreYa

http://www.storeya.com/ebay-to-facebook. StoreYa places a tab on your Facebook fan page so you can begin selling immediately. They also have apps that support Shopify, Amazon, Magneto, and WordPress among others.

3D Sellers

http://apps.ebay.com/selling?ViewEAppDetails&stab=3&appType=1&appId=SocialStore.3dsellers.com. Social Store from 3D

Sellers is available in the eBay apps center and lets you add your eBay store to your Facebook fan page.

Boost your Facebook Post

Sometimes your Facebook posts needs a little more oomph to reach more viewers.

I know what you're thinking. "Hey! I'm on Facebook because it's free. What do you mean I have to spend money to get my posts seen?"

I know, it's crazy but it's true. Facebook has created a new way to make money, and part of it involves hiding your posts, or as they would have it—strategically placing them towards the top of a user's News Feed, if you kick in a minor contribution to Zuckerberg and Company.

Before I tell you how to boost your post, I'm going to share what Facebook says about boosting your post. *Boosted posts appear higher in your News Feed, so there's a better chance you will see them.*

You can boost any type of post—video, picture, or text. To boost a post, click on Boost post in the lower left hand corner of the post. After you do that, select the audience demographics you want to see your post, your budget, and the length of time to boost the post.

Pretty simple so far, right?

In most cases, five to fifteen dollars should get you a big enough boost to reach your audience. If it's something really special, like a new product launch, maybe budget forty or fifty dollars. As for the audience, try to narrow the focus to your prime demographic. If it's showing your message is targeted to millions of readers try to narrow it down some. Shoot for something in the range of fifty to one hundred thousand for your target audience. For your time frame you have a choice of one to seven days. If you boost it longer than two or three days you're going to find yourself pushing old news.

Create a Facebook Event to Promote Your Sale

A Facebook event may or may not work for you. The reason I say this is you can only create an event from your personal Facebook page, not from your Facebook fan page.

Don't get discouraged yet.

Promoting an event to your regular Facebook friends can help you introduce a new product line, or try out new ideas you normally wouldn't use with your regular customers.

Think of your event as a marketing test? It's a chance for you to try new things, and for your friends to get a hell of a deal. Promote it to them that way, and it will be a win-win situation for both of you.

If you're unfamiliar with Facebook events, the easiest way to think of it is as an online party invite. I've received them for family reunions, book launch events, and birthday parties.

The great thing about creating a Facebook event is once you set it up, it does all the work for you. It sends out the invites, collects RSVPs, and posts a reminder on the Facebook homepage for everyone who was invited.

The other cool thing is a Facebook event is super easy to create and manage.

Final takeaway

Facebook can be a great way to help grow your business. Like anything else it can become a bottomless pit sucking up all of your time if you're not careful.

To be successful selling on Facebook you need to

1. Have a plan. Know what you want to accomplish. Do you want to make more sales? Encourage email sign ups? Engage more with customers?
2. Budget 15 to 20 minutes a day three or four days a week and stick to that time limit.
3. Be visual. Facebook users respond best to videos and pictures. Give them what they want, and you will be more successful.
4. Don't over-post, or under-post. If you post too often users are going to unfollow you, or turn off your News Feed. If you don't post often enough, people are going to forget who you are. Three to five good posts a week is enough to get your message out there.

5. Spend a few bucks to boost your posts, especially when you're first getting started. It will help you build your audience faster.
6. Find an app, and add your eBay store to your Facebook fan page.
7. If you have an email list, link to your sign up form. If you don't have an email list—what are you waiting for?

Twitter

For those of you not familiar with Twitter, it's the social media site with the little blue bird as its symbol. When you feel compelled to communicate with the outside world, you send out a *tweet.*

Tweets are short, sweet, and to the point. There's no room for fluff or excess verbiage. You get 140 characters to tell your story, so you better boil it down to the essentials, and make every character count.

The other cool thing about Twitter is you can share pictures, videos, and links. In fact, if you don't include some visual element in each of your tweets, the odds are no one is going to bother with them. Sorry, but that's another rule of the game you're going to need to get used to.

. . . .

On the face of things, Twitter would appear to be the easiest social media site to master. I mean, you only have 140 characters to work with. All you need to do is punch them out, click send, and your story is let loose upon the world.

If only it were so simple.

The way Twitter works, your message is only seen by your followers and other Twitter users with nothing better to do than search the Twitterverse all day for trending topics.

Your topic is trending, isn't it?

We'll get to that in a bit. For now the very least you need to know is Twitter is one of the social medial powerhouses. According to Twitter they have 288 million users who send out 500 million tweets each and every day. Many of these users send out as many as fifty to one hundred tweets per day.

Twitter's about page gives us two other key pieces of intelligence.

1. 80 percent of Twitter users visit the site via mobile. That means every tweet you send needs to be mobile friendly, and every link you include in your tweets needs to look good on the small screen of a smartphone or iPhone.

2. 77 percent of Twitter users are outside of the United States which means there is a potentially huge communications gap. Many of the people who receive your tweets aren't going to understand what you're saying, so the visual element better tell your entire story. It if doesn't, you're wasting your time.

With that many tweets going out every day you can understand how easy it is to get lost in the clutter. Later in this section I'll give you some tips to cut through the noise, and make your tweets easier to find.

Twitter 101

Twitter is a form of microblogging.

Conversations on Twitter take place in real time and whittle the conversation down to short 140 character bursts.

The advantage to users is that it is instantaneous and occurs in real time. A lot of the breaking news stories you see on Headline News are broken on Twitter.

Here's the scenario. A lone gunman attacks a school or business. Trapped students capture footage on their cell phones and post it to Twitter. Moments later it's picked up by network news and spread across the media.

Another scenario that plays out every year during storm season is someone captures footage of a tornado roaring by their home as they're headed for the storm cellar. Minutes later the video hits Twitter, then it's uploaded to Facebook, the local news station's website, and next thing you know there's a viral video of the storm tossing a car into a tree or the house next door.

That's the instantaneous nature of Twitter. As soon as something happens, you can have it online within seconds.

The good thing is disaster videos aren't the only ones that go viral. You can shoot a quick video of a dog chasing a note pinned to its tail, kids going crazy flinging mud or snowballs, or even of a staged accident or event at work.

The Least You Need to Know

You can open a personal or business Twitter account. There is very little difference between the two.

Next you need to edit your profile. A lot of businesses skip this step.

Big mistake!

At the very least you need to add your company name, contact info, links to your blog—website, or other social media accounts, a profile photo, and a short one line bio. Other than your contact info the most important stuff you enter here is your bio. It tells people who you are, why you're on Twitter, and how you can help them.

My author bio on Twitter is short, sweet, and says all you need to know about me—"Short easy to read solutions to your ecommerce problems."

My eBay Twitter bio takes the same approach—"Unique historical memorabilia covering the period from 1850 to 1970—magazine articles, newspapers, and vintage advertisements."

It's just 128 characters long, but gives readers a good idea of what I'm all about. Create your bio the same way. Twitter gives you 160 characters to introduce yourself, make an impression, and convince visitors to click on your links. Spend the time you need to craft an amazing bio.

Here's one other piece of advice. If you run a brick and mortar location as well as an eBay business focus on local. Let's say you're selling custom blended coffees in Seattle. Let people know you're located in Seattle. Depending on your business image make it snarky. "Unlike that other big name Seattle coffee shop, most coffee drinkers say our coffee packs a punch and doesn't drain your wallet." It's only 125 characters, but it tells your story, lets readers know you're not afraid to take on the big kid on the block, and hints that they won't have to ante up five bucks for a cup of java.

Overall, it gives readers a good impression of your business that may make them want to learn a little more about you.

Twitter also gives you an opportunity to upload a theme to help brand your page.

Twitter recommends 1500 x 500 pixels as the ideal size for your header, but you can upload any theme you like between the sizes of 1024 x 280 pixels and 2560 x 600 pixels. You can get all of the details by following this link. http://ct-social.com/twitter-header-template-2014/. You will also find a header template, and directions to help create an amazing header.

Getting Started

As I said earlier, tweets need to be short, sweet, and on target. You need to boil your message down to one quick point. That means you need to do a little planning before you start clicking the keys on your keyboard.

The first thing you need to do is select a tool to shorten the link you're going to use in your tweet. Two tools I recommend are **bitly** https://bitly.com/shorten/ and **Google URL Shortener** https://goo.gl/.

Here's an eBay URL for an Otterbox iPhone 6 case.

http://www.ebay.com/itm/NEW-Otterbox-Defender-Commuter-Symmetry-Case-for-Apple-iPhone-6-Plus-5-5-/321639090877?pt=LH_DefaultDomain_0&var=&hash=item4ae32f0abd

Here's the same link after it's been run through **bitly**.

http://ebay.to/1xZQSsC

See the difference?

If you used the original link it's 156 characters. That's more than you're allowed for your entire tweet. After bitly performs its magic, your link is down to a svelte 23 characters. That leaves plenty of characters to craft an amazing tweet.

Here's an example.

Let's say you're running a big sale on iPhone 6 Otterbox cases this week, and you want to let potential buyers know about it. You could just blurt it out –

Large selection of iPhone 6 Otterbox Cases starting at $29.99 http://ebay.to/1xZQSsC

That's good. But, it doesn't really move anyone to take action.

What we need to do is rework it using more action words that motivate readers to take action on your message.

Try this one on for size.

Refurbished iPhone 6 Otterbox case. Guaranteed to protect your iPhone. 2 days only. Starts at $29.99. Check them out. http://ebay.to/1xZQSsC

The entire tweet is just 139 characters, but it does everything you want it to. It tells potential buyers why (guaranteed to protect your iPhone), it includes a call to action (2 days only), and it gives the price (Starts at $29.99).

Not bad!

That's what you need to do with every tweet you send out.

1. Boil your message down to just the essentials.
2. Use action words wherever possible.
3. Include a call to action.

An even better way to approach your Otterbox promotion would be to include a link to an installation or review video, and add links to your sale items or eBay store. It's less salesy, and will focus more eyes on your tweet.

Here's another surprising factoid you need to consider. The shorter your tweet, the more likely it is to be read.

Research shows short tweets—between 80 to 100 characters are the most effective, and tend to get read the most.

That means the less you say, the more effective your tweet is going to be.

Lesson learned.

K. I. S. S.

Keep it simple stupid!

#Hashtags# - The Art of Getting Found

Getting found on Twitter revolves around using hashtags—better known as the # sign.

If you want to boil Twitter SEO down to the bare bones—this is it. Hashtags are nothing more than searchable keywords. When you use a hashtag it makes it easier for other Twitter users to find your content.

Here are a few examples of hashtags currently used on Twitter.

- #CocaCola
- #MylieCyrus
- #ValentinesDay
- #WorldSeries
- #iPhone6
- #SuperBowlChampions

As you can see, hashtags are nothing more than keywords proceeded by the # sign. Sometimes users include more than one hashtag in a tweet: #Beatles #John #Paul #George #Ringo. You're not breaking any Twitter rules by using multiple hashtags, but I'd suggest keeping it to no more than two. Anymore, and readers are going to think you're screaming for attention, or suffering from a bad case of keyword spamming syndrome.

Now that you know what hashtags are, let's take a look at how to use them.

The first thing to remember is you only want to use hashtags that are relevant to your business. Miley Cyrus is popular, and tweeting about her will get your tweet a lot of views, but if it puts the wrong eyes on your tweets it's not going to do you any good.

Let's take my eBay business for example. At first glance old magazine articles aren't very sexy, or at the top of Twitter's trending list. But, if I position them correctly—they are relevant to a certain segment of the Twitterverse.

Try these tweets on for size, and pay special attention to the hashtags.

- Vintage magazine cover #MartinLutherKing assassination. Only one available.

- Original newspaper #AbrahamLincoln inauguration. Last day, bid now.

- Indian account of #CustersLastStand. Originally published in 1898. Make it yours.

- #VintageMoviePoster #GoneWithTheWind. One of kind collectible. Bid now.

- #HistoricalCollectibles #IowaHistory #AmanaColonies Largest selection anywhere.

Most of my posts follow the rule of one hashtag per tweet, but every now and then I break the rule because my content appeals to several different market segments.

Another thing you will notice is most of my hashtags come in the center of the tweet, rather than at the beginning. It's counterintuitive to what you'd think, but recent research shows placing the hashtag in the center of the tweet is more effective. I'm not sure why, but it seems to work. Test it for yourself to see if it boosts your response rate.

Several of my tweets also include a call to action—"Bid now." "Only one available." "Make it yours." "Last day." They're subtle hints to let readers know, you better act now, because this offer isn't going to last long.

Other businesses create a unique hashtag that includes their business name. It can be as simple as your name - #MoneyBagsPayDayLoans, or it can be a slogan - #BatteriesForLess. It may be a tag to help people discover your local business #QuadCityMagician or #DavenportDJ.

Whatever you decide for your hashtag strategy the key is to make it relevant. Choose hashtags that will help your business get discovered. If you're unsure whether a hashtag is a good fit for your business or not, run a search on Twitter and see what pops up.

Get Followed – How to Build Your Tribe

There's a lot of advice floating around about how to build your follower base. Some of it is good, some of it not so good. The reason I say this is a lot of the *gurus* endorse the more is better syndrome. Paris Hilton has ten trillion followers so you need to get that many too.

That's not quite true.

Sean Platt, Johnny B. Truant, and David Wright put it best in their book, **Write. Publish. Repeat**. To be successful you only need one thousand true fans. Their book is about building your career as an author, but the advice applies to any business trying to build a social media platform or fan base.

It doesn't take a bazillion followers to build your business. It just takes one thousand *true fans* who will buy every new product you release, and tell their friends.

Contrast this with the typical advice you're going to find about building followers on Twitter.

Here's the way it goes.

Make a list of the big players in your field. Start following their followers. If after two days they don't follow you back, unfollow them. Rinse and repeat. Over time you will amass a large list of followers.

Don't get me wrong. It's an effective strategy, and it has worked well for many businesses that want to develop a massive number of followers. But, if you're a business, it's not about the number of followers you have, it's about the number of followers who will become customers and take action on your tweets.

Don't work harder than you have to.

Post eight to ten solid tweets a week. Offer valuable content your followers will enjoy and use. Keep the amount of self-promotion to a minimum. For every ten tweets you shoot out, no more than one or two should be salesy. If your followers get even the slightest hint you're more interested in selling to them than sharing with them they're going to unfollow you.

The key to success on Twitter is to provide great content that encourages readers to check out your bio and contact links. If you continue to provide pertinent content the sales will follow.

I know this has been said before, but social media marketing is more of a marathon than a sprint. Short bursts will get you attention, but staying in the game over the long haul is how you win.

Pinterest

Pinterest is nothing more than a ginormous virtual bulletin board. Users find things they like, and pin them on their own board. After they've done that the magic begins to happen. Other users stumble across their pins, and can re-pin them on their boards eventually sharing them with thousands of online viewers around the world.

Another way to think of Pinterest is to look at it as a virtual scrapbook where you can store (pin) all of your favorite things. The cool part is you don't need scissors, paste, or tape to put it together. Just click your mouse and your content is stored away, and ready for friends and strangers to check it all out.

Pinterest is actually a number of applications packed into one. It is a –

1. Social media site

2. Social bookmarking hub

3. Content curation tool

The really exciting thing about Pinterest though, is it was designed to be more visually oriented right out of the box. That gives it a huge advantage over Facebook and Twitter. Unlike Zuckerberg and Company Pinterest doesn't have to retrofit their site to catch up. Instead they're forcing the big guns like Facebook to reengineer their timeline to make it more visually oriented.

The other thing Pinterest has going for it compared to other social media sites is it works.

I have hundreds of bookmarks I pinned on three Pinterest boards over two years ago, and they are still being re-pinned fifteen to twenty times per week. Try to get that kind of traction with Facebook or Twitter. It's not going to happen. Most posts made on those sites have a shelf life of a few hours to a few days.

The Least You Need to Know

When you sign up Pinterest shows a prompt where you can register as a business user, rather than as an individual. The easiest way to brand your business on Pinterest is to fill out your about section as completely as possible.

Use your business email address when you sign up. Choose the business type closest to your own. A little farther on down the page you get the opportunity to set up your business profile. If it's not already taken by another user select your business name. If it's not available try to pick something similar to it or another name that people associate with your business. Include your contact name if you would like visitors to your boards to know who you are.

There is also a spot for a picture. You can use your logo, or a shot of one of your products, but a better choice would be a picture of yourself. It will help visitors connect with you.

Below this you will see a section labeled *about you*. It gives your 160 characters to tell visitors all about you, and why they should do business with you. Again, don't sell. Use appropriate keywords that compel viewers to find out more about you. "Featuring historical collectibles from 1806 to 1970—magazines, newspapers, and historical prints." Or, "Custom presentation folders designed to wow your clients—because first impressions really do count."

If you're a local business with a brick and mortar location include your city, state, or region, whichever is more beneficial to your business. You're also able to add a website URL. If you don't have a website, copy and paste the link for your eBay or Amazon store.

Towards the bottom of the information you can include links to your various social media sites—Facebook, Twitter, Google+, and your Yahoo and Gmail accounts.

Getting Started

Getting started on Pinterest is about as easy as it gets. From the home screen click the plus sign in the box where it says *create board*. The board setup screen pops up next. First, it asks you to name your board. The skies the limit when it comes to names, but you can get a bigger bang for your buck if you use strong keywords in your board's name. If your board is about early American magazines, you could name it "Illustrated History of Early American Magazines from 1857 to 1899."

If it's a board detailing Theodore Roosevelt in the Spanish American War you could name it, "Theodore Roosevelt in the Spanish American War—San Juan Hill, Rough Riders." Doing it this way gives viewers three more opportunities to find it than just saying "Theodore Roosevelt" or the "Spanish American War."

Next up is the description box. You have 160 characters to tell everyone what your board is about. Be clear, concise, and load it with appropriate keywords. After this you need to choose a category for your board. Pick the one that is closet to your topic.

I've Created My First Board, Now What?

Congratulations! You created your first board, now what do you do?

That's a situation most users face every time they start a new board. What it really comes down to is what you expect to accomplish with your board. Do you want to get a ton of new followers? Do you want to drive traffic to your website? Or is your goal to direct people to your eBay store?

Give this question some thought before you start pinning, because certain types of pins will create certain types of reactions on the part of your viewers. If you sell cellular phone accessories on eBay the ultimate goal is probably to drive traffic to your eBay store, but if all you post is links to items you have for sale, it's going to scare people away. They're going to think you're being to salesy. You need to take a more balanced approach. For every one or two store items you pin to your board, pin eight to ten links to stories about new phones and products.

The idea is to give viewers a wide variety of information centered around products they enjoy. Pin technical articles about how to reset their email, or product recall notifications. If you have your own blog or website, that's even better. Send viewers to content you've written, that way they're more likely to stumble across links to your eBay store, mail list, and other items you're selling.

The main thing is to stay focused. Don't pin pictures of your kids or your pets, no matter how cute you think they are. Your board is about your business and for it to do its job you need to keep focused.

When you pin items make sure you write a strong keyword loaded description. Also, when you're posting pictures or videos make sure you link to the source article or page so viewers can hyperlink to the original source.

Optimal picture size on Pinterest is 500 pixels wide x 600 pixels high—taller pictures display better, so whenever possible try to post taller images.

Keep in mind you're not limited to just posting pictures or links, you can also pin videos from YouTube, Vimeo, and other streaming sites. If you're having trouble getting your stuff re-pinned video will set your boards on fire.

Here are a few other tips to help make your pins more effective.

1. You can add a price to your pins by adding a dollar sign or pound sign in the description. When you do this Pinterest will display the price in the upper left corner of your pin.

2. Pinterest is similar to Twitter in that you can use hashtags to make items more searchable. Again, don't go overboard with your hashtags—using #yummy or #wow won't help your pins get found.

3. If you have a website or blog you can add the Pin-it button to make it easier for users to share your content.

4. Don't use just one board. Create a number of different boards keyed to different user interests. That way your pins can be more focused, and more effective.

5. Female users outnumber male users by almost four to one so use soft colors, tone down your language, and post pictures and videos directed towards women.

YouTube

Video will set your eBay business apart more than any other thing you do because no one is doing it.

They're scared.

They don't understand it. So they don't do it.

That spells opportunity for you and me.

Here's the low down: *Adults aged eighteen to thirty-four tune into YouTube more than they do any single cable television network. YouTube is the place millennials go for digital content.*

More than one billion visitors flock to YouTube every day. Three hundred hours of video are uploaded to YouTube every minute. Sixty percent of your viewers will come from outside of your home country. And, more than half of You Tube views are mobile.

If you still have doubts about whether you should be posting videos on YouTube consider this. YouTube is the third most visited website on the internet, and the second most used search engine. And, since YouTube is owned by Google videos posted there rank high in Google search.

How to Use YouTube

1. Include a short video in each of your listings that introduces your business, and tells potential customers more about you, your products, and how you do business. Checkout Fiverr celebrity Professor Puppet as he introduces my eBay business—history-bytes. https://www.youtube.com/watch?v=tVt6YlF_4hw.

2. Create short how-to guides that show how to use the products you're selling, how to hook it up, or how to maintain it. Here's a link to a short video showing how to install the Otterbox Defender case on the iPhone 6. https://www.youtube.com/watch?v=hjl5NkrbgiE.

3. Review the products you're selling. Tell viewers what you like about the product, why you like it, what you don't like, and how it stacks up against the competition. When you do this, make sure you place the video on YouTube and in your product listing on eBay.

4. Share industry news. If you sell food service equipment and you just spent the week at NACS, or another regional show let viewers know about the awesome new ovens or food products you saw. Snag an interview with company reps or show officials. Every time you do this it will build your authority as an expert in your field.

What to Do in Your Video

Think of YouTube as a personal invite into a viewer's home. When they choose to watch your video they're inviting you into their home for a personal chat.

Make the most of it.

Use this opportunity to share your knowledge. Even if you don't think of yourself as an expert; chances are you know more than ninety percent of the people who are going to watch your video.

Be yourself.

Approach it like you're talking to a friend. If you're filming an introduction to your business the easiest way to do it is to sit at a table surrounded by some of the products you sell.

Introduce your business.

Tell people how long you've been in business, what got you started, and why you're so passionate about it. Point to a few of your products, or pick them up and tell viewers what's so great about them.

Chances are after the first ten or fifteen seconds the nervousness will go away, and you will catch yourself thinking, "Why was I ever scared of this?" I know that's the way I felt after filming my first video book review for Amazon. I'd been planning to do it for a year but always found an excuse to put it off. Once I finished the first one I realized it was a cakewalk— just point the camera, and start talking.

Here are three tips to keep in mind when making your video.

1. Don't try to sell from your video. Focus on providing great content. If it's what people want, they will checkout your links and visit your eBay store, email sign up form, or social media sites.

2. Be consistent. Focus on a single topic—old books, baseball cards, GI Joe, Manga, or Anime. It's easier to build an audience when your content focuses around one topic. If you try to cover too many topics, viewers will become confused and look for more content elsewhere.

3. Keep it conversational. The best videos are relaxed—just you chatting with friends.

Necessary Equipment

Chances are you already have all of the equipment needed to get started posting YouTube videos.

Your smartphone or iPhone camera can capture higher resolution video than a high end camcorder from several years ago. If you have an iPad or other tablet, most models come equipped with one or two high resolution video cameras. Barring that many YouTubers flip open their laptop and shoot video directly from the built-in video camera.

Most experts agree sound is the key to a good video. Because of the limitations imposed by built-in microphones most videographers suggest purchasing an external microphone. You can find good quality mics on eBay or Amazon for fifty to one hundred dollars.

One final word of advice on sound—make sure you have something to say. You don't have to script the whole video out. That's the surest way to chase viewers away if you just sit there and read a canned script. The best thing to do is jot down a few talking points, and glance down at them for help when you find yourself stumbling over what to say next.

Lighting is another key ingredient to making a great video.

I shot my first view video sitting in a recliner next to a table lamp. I just held my iPhone at arm's length and started talking. The end result was okay, but you could tell the lighting was off. Everything was sort of dark and shadowy.

There are a couple of ways to approach lighting.

The least expensive method is to film in areas where there is plenty of natural light. Outdoors is great in season. Barring that you can open the window shades and shoot your video in the open light.

If you have some extra money to toss around you can set up an indoor studio. A desk or table surrounded by the products you sell would make an ideal background setting. You can pick up some flood lights or photography lights so you always have the proper lighting. That way you can film day or night without any worries.

The final piece of equipment you need is an inexpensive tripod.

If you're shooting a short one or two minute video it's not too hard to hold your iPhone steady, but when your video starts to run five, ten minutes, or more you're going to find it hard to hold your arm steady. And, wait until the first time you try holding a product in one hand and your iPhone in the other. Something has to give, and the odds are your hand is going to start shaking.

A tripod makes filming your video easier over the long haul. You don't have to worry about sudden movements, and when you want to hold up a product or move around it's a whole lot easier when you use a tripod.

In time you may want to dress things up a bit.

There is a lot of good video editing software available. Windows Movie Maker is free from Microsoft and relatively easy to use. There are several video editing apps available for the iPhone and Android phones. Visit the apps store to check out what's available.

If you plan to record screen shots Camtasia or Snagit will do a good job for you. Another option is to use PowerPoint and post a slide show from it.

Shooting Your First Video

Don't worry that your first video isn't perfect. Just make it. Everybody's first video looks like it was created by an amateur. It's okay. Your videos will get better over time. Six months or a year from now when you re-watch your first few videos you will realize they're not as bad as you thought. Here's a fact you might as well get used to: you're usually your own worst critic.

Here's a simple structure for your videos.

1. First 10 to 15 seconds. Say what you're going to do, and let viewers know why they should watch it.

   Here are a few quick ways to start your video.

   "This short video is going to cover the early history of Harper's Weekly Magazine from 1850 to 1876…" or "This short video is going to introduce you to the 1955 Topps Baseball card set, and help you recognize common grading problems."

2. 15 to 30 seconds. Tell them what's in it for them. "Harper's Weekly was published in one and two volume annual sets so it's important you know the details before making any purchase." "One of the problems with the 1955 Topps Baseball sets is scammers often trim the margins to make the card appear better than it is."

3. 60 to 180 seconds. Start talking. Deliver the information you promised in short easy bursts. Whenever possible

illustrate what you're talking about with stories and anecdotes.

4. 10 to 15 seconds. Recap what you talked about. Tell them what you talked about, why it's important, and what you want them to do next. Watch the next video in your series. Sign up for your email list, or check out your item on eBay.

Whatever you do, don't try to sell directly from your video. YouTube lets you add links in your description below the video. If your video is good enough, viewers will check out your links. Some may even visit your eBay store listings—who knows, they may even buy something.

That brings us to setting up your video on YouTube.

The title and description are essential to your video getting found in search. If you do it right you will get thousands of extra views.

The title of your YouTube video serves the same purpose as the title of your eBay listing. It powers the site's search engine.

Keywords are king.

Your main keyword should be the first or second keyword in your title.

Example:

- Thomas Nast Santa Claus Illustrations in Harper's Weekly Magazine.
- Installing the Otterbox Defender Case on the iPhone 6
- 1954 Topps Baseball Inserts in Sports Illustrated Magazine

Another way to approach your title is to pose the questions you plan to answer in your video .

Example:

- Frequently Asked Questions About the 1955 Topps Baseball Card Set
- What to Look for When You Grade Old Books and Magazines
- Why You Should Have Second Thoughts About Purchasing an iPhone on Craigslist

It's also important to sprinkle keywords throughout the description of your video. YouTube gives you 1,000 characters to craft your description so be sure you get it right.

Write naturally.

Your description should mirror your video. Tell viewers what it's about, why they need to watch it, what they will learn by watching it, and what you want them to do next. Include at least one link at the bottom of your description. It can be to your eBay store, your mail list signup form, or your social media sites.

The key is not to sell.

Provide links to your store, or wherever you have your items for sale. If your content is good enough viewers will make the next move and visit your store. You don't have to push them.

Tags help YouTube determine who to show your video to. Make sure to include the appropriate keywords in your tags. If you're in doubt about which ones to include check out your competition, and borrow from them.

And, here's one final tip.

Those in the know say Google transcribes videos to search for appropriate keywords so be sure to include your keywords in the context of your video.

Final Takeaway

To get the best response you should make several different types of videos. Nothing personal, but people are going to get tired of watching your videos if they're all of just you talking. To be effective you've got to shake things up now and then.

Here are some of the different types of video you should consider.

1. Talking head. Just like it sounds, you point the camera and people watch you talking from the shoulders up. It's the easiest type of video to make, and often the most effective if done right. Be yourself. Be natural. And, make sure the camera is adjusted properly so you don't chop the top of your head off.

2. Testimonials. Get some of your customers to hop in front of the camera and talk about the items you sell, or why they like doing business with you. Remember you can tell people and tell people how good you are, but it's more effective when someone else tells why they like to do business with you.

3. Screen capture. This is pretty easy stuff. Capture the actions you're making on the computer screen while doing a voice over explaining them. Done properly these videos can be very effective, especially when you're doing computer tutorials.

4. Walk about. Take your camera and walk around your business. Introduce some of your key employees while they're doing their job. Catch someone asleep on the job, or goofing off. Maybe Dave and Sharon sing at break or when they're packaging shipments. There are several ways of doing this. Make it serious, or capture the goofy moments.

5. FAQs. Sit down at your desk and answer common questions about your business—shipping fees, combined shipments, returns, how items are packed, and how soon

customers can expect to receive their order after hitting the buy button.

Google +

Google + isn't as big as Facebook (yet), but they have something better going for them. They're a part of the Google family, and posts placed there rank instantly in search.

For this reason alone, it's hard not to be on Google +.

They also have some nifty features the other guys don't. Among these are Hangouts, and Businesses Pages that integrate into Google search.

If you're still unconvinced why you should be on Google + consider this—if you're a local business unable to shell out big bucks for advertising, and unable to compete with the big guys, Google + and Google Local Business can propel you to the top of search listings in your city, region, or state.

Google Hangouts gives you the opportunity to conference one-on-one with clients and potential customers from your neck-of-the-woods, or from around the world.

What that means is even though you're a management consultant working from your home office or kitchen table, you can consult with clients around the world. You can conduct a one-on-one conversation with them, or chat with a small group of potential clients.

For eBay sellers the advantage is just as great.

A Google +Business Page can help move your business to the top of search. It puts all of your info out there for everyone to see. And more importantly it helps potential customers connect with you by filling in the missing gaps. On eBay and Amazon buyers see what you're selling, but they don't get to meet the person behind the products.

Google + changes everything by sharing more information about you. When you set up a Business Page you get to tell your story—what you do, why you do it, and how you can add value to your customer's purchasing experience. You can also include links to your ecommerce sites, social media pages, blogs, websites, etc.

Hangouts give sellers the opportunity to brand themselves and build authority in their field.

Let's say you sell vintage baseball cards on eBay. Maybe you've got a good business going, but you want to do better. With hangouts you could invite select groups of clients to hop online with you for a short video conference where you discuss how to grade the 1955 Topps Baseball Set, or maybe you could talk about the importance of the 1954 and 1955 baseball inserts in Sports Illustrated Magazine.

Each talk gives you the opportunity to up your value and expertise level in the eyes of your clients.

Hundreds of sellers offer vintage baseball cards on eBay and Amazon. Imagine how potential customers will react if you take the time to communicate one-on-one with them to provide them with the information they want and need to enhance their collections and expand their personal knowledge base.

I know what you're thinking. Yeah! It's a great way to connect with customers, but who's got the time! I have a full time job. In my spare time I have to scan pictures, write product descriptions, and mail out what I sold overnight.

It's a battle. It really is. Everything is competing for your valuable time, and here I am suggesting you spend time doing face-to-face videos with customers and potential customers.

I must be some kind of nutcase, right?

Maybe. Maybe not.

Let's talk a little more about Google +, and we can come back to this later when the time is right.

Getting Started with Google +

Google + (or Google Plus) is the new kid on the block in social media. Because they're backed by the power of Google they have quickly become the number two player in the game second only to Facebook with 400 million registered users.

In essence Google + is Facebook on steroids because Google integrates information from Plus into search. If searchers insert a (+) before their search term it pulls up a list of Google + Business Pages. If you operate a brick and mortar location along with your online store Google + is a must have for your business.

The easiest way to get started with Google + is to sign up with your Gmail address.

Keep in mind, you can't just start a Business Page on Google +. You need to set up a personal page first. One other thing you need to know, Google requires you to open your Plus account with your real name. Anonymity is not allowed.

Your Google + profile consists of three separate pieces of information.

1. Picture
2. Bio
3. Contact Info

Use a professional photo appropriate to your business. If you're a lawyer by all means wear a suit; if you run a web store, blue jeans, t-shirt, and sandals may be just the ticket; and if you're a clown, make sure to wear that big old red nose, plenty of make-up, and orange hair.

Next you're asked to provide your bio or story.

Your story starts with a *tagline*. If you're a local business, you need to work your location into your wordage.

- Quad-City Plumber
- Mid-West Based Ecommerce Author
- Davenport Iowa Antiquarian Bookseller

My tagline on Google + is "short easy to read solutions to your ecommerce problems." It's a perfect introduction, and tells everyone exactly what I do.

Under this you will find a spot for your *introduction*. This is where you make your pitch; tell people what you do; and why you're the guy to solve their problem. You've got as much space as you like to tell your story, but shorter is probably better. People have a short attention span, especially on the internet.

To give you an idea of what to say, I posted my Amazon author bio in my introduction.

My books offer short easy to read solutions to your ecommerce problems.

Most of them can be read in under an hour. The information can be used to help you sell more products on eBay and Amazon, services on Fiverr, or eBooks on Amazon and Kindle.

Selling on line isn't a mystery. It doesn't even have to be difficult.

It's really all about getting started. Many people I've talked with have this crazy fear about putting things up for sale on eBay and Amazon. They think they have to do this and do that; they worry they don't know enough about what they're doing to do it right; they wonder what they should sell; and they worry about whether they can even do it or not.

That's where my books come in.

They take you hand-in-hand and walk you through getting started selling on eBay, Amazon, and Fiverr. They show you how to market your Kindle book.

My goal is to help you over the speed bumps, so you can be more successful from the get-go.

What are you waiting for?

Most of my books are available as audio books, so if you prefer to listen rather than read, be sure to check them out.

Just below this there's a section called *bragging rights*. You can talk about your kids, your prize American Eskimo puppy, awards or honors you've received, or volunteer work. Choose something that will make you stand out with your audience.

As an online business work and educational background may or may not be relevant to your profile. If you're a self-employed artist selling your art online, a mention of your BFA or MFA, or residency in a distinguished art program could be a huge plus. If you sell party supplies, education is probably not a deciding factor in your profile. Do what you think is best. *Tip: There is a check box to the right of each question where you can choose who sees your information. That way you can make your work and educational background available on a need-to-know basis.*

Contact information lets viewers know how they can get in touch with you. I'd suggest erring on the cautious side here. An email address is probably safe. If you have a separate business phone feel free to share it here. Unless you have a separate brick and mortar location I wouldn't provide an address outside of city, state, or region. There are a lot of disturbed individuals on the internet, no sense in putting yourself on their radar unnecessarily.

Basic information collects your gender (male / female), information on the type of connections you're looking for (networking / personal / clients), birthdate, relationship (are you married / dating / a little too personal here), and any other names you go by (keep it appropriate for your audience).

Links is a way to help viewers connect with you. Be sure to include links to your website, blog, eBay and Amazon store, and any other social media sites you are on.

. . . .

Setting up a separate Business Page is similar to setting up your Google + personal page, only this time you're going to slant the information towards your business.

When you set up your business page you want to make sure you link your business website to your Google + Business Page. When you do this it will always bring your website to the front of search. *Tip: If you don't have a business website link to your eBay or Amazon storefront.*

Earlier I mentioned Hangouts, a spot where you can hold real time video chats with up to nine of your contacts. Google + has several other unique features you need to know about.

Your contacts are separated into groups labeled Circles. When you first get started on Google + they suggest four circles—friends, family, acquaintances, and following.

You can add as many circles as you like. Just be aware you are limited to 5,000 persons total in all of your circles.

You're in charge of who is in your circles, and people can be in more than one circle. It all depends upon how you classify them.

The idea is to group similar contacts together. When you do this it makes it easier to share information, because you can limit who receives which message. If you're an online seller you could setup a number of different circles coordinated to how many purchases buyers have made, or by the type of merchandise they have purchased. This way you can send targeted messages to each group, or if you're really ambitious you could create several different newsletters targeted at each group of customers.

There are two different ways to add people to circles: add a person, and type a name. The add a person option is only available on personal pages.

Add a person lets you search for someone by name or email address. If the person you want to add isn't on Google +, Google will email them an invitation so they can join and connect with you. *Tip: You don't have to know the person you invite to connect with you. So go ahead. Fire off an invitation to Barrack Obama or Taylor Swift; just don't be offended if they don't take time out to add you back. Type a name* is how you search for people to add to your Circles on a Business Page.

Similar to Facebook you can like or unlike people (Circle and un-Circle). To un-Circle someone highlight them, and click on the *remove* link. If one of your contacts gets out of line and you don't want to un-Circle them, you can block them. It's sort of like clapping a set of earplugs on them; they can no longer follow your conversation.

You can call people out or mention them by putting an * @ * or * + *in front of their user name. For example, @BarrackObama or +BarrackObama. The difference is when you use +BarrackObama the person is notified that you mentioned them. Using +username is a good way to grab someone's attention and make sure you get noticed.

Google+ also has a messaging service for members that is much faster than texting. Instant upload saves all of your pictures from your phone to a private area on Google+. The only drawback is the feature is only available to Android users. Take that Apple.

A quick way to search out users on Google + is to use the search bar. It's located under the menu bar at the top of the page to the right of the Google+ logo. You can search for people or businesses the same way. When you click on a displayed name it takes you to their Google+ page.

Google+ also has a feature called communities. A community is a group of like-minded people who hang out and share their knowledge. Feel free to join a community, or if you don't see one that fits your tastes you can start your own community.

Going back to Hangouts—up to nine people can hold an online video conference. If you have people in your hangout who speak a different language, you can engage Google translate to make communication easier. Another great thing about Hangouts is you can post and share documents or doodle on a shared sketch board.

Hangouts are an excellent way for online sellers to enhance their authority, develop their customer list, and build interest in high dollar items.

Let's say you sell vintage sports collectibles. You could run a series of Hangouts focusing on grading different sets, common forgeries, and investment grade collectibles. If you have a one of a kind collectible you will be offering online you can build interest in the weeks leading up to the sale by hosting a series of Hangouts that feature the collectible, document its history, and talk about previous owners.

The skies the limit with Google +.

You can brand yourself as an expert, share facts about your online business, or use video – pictures – and chat to strengthen the connection with your customers.

What are you waiting for?

LinkedIn

LinkedIn is the world's largest network of professional and business users. It has over 200 million register users worldwide with a targeted income of over $100,000 per year. They are college educated, and tend to be older than users on other social networks—the average age is between 50 and 65. Another thing to keep in mind is sixty percent of LinkedIn users come from outside of the United States, so you're going to be working with a large international audience.

How important LinkedIn is as a social network for online sellers is directly related to the products you sell.

If you're a service oriented business offering resume writing, cover letters, and job coaching tips LinkedIn would be a perfect match for your target audience. If you approach it right LinkedIn could also be a great audience for sellers offering any type of high end products—gourmet food and beverages, electronics, audio, planners, etc.

For sellers of low end consumables like mid-range fashions, CDs, DVDs, and commodity type food products, the value of LinkedIn is debatable.

If you sell commodity and other low end products I'd use LinkedIn to build connections with other sellers, suppliers, and industry experts. This way you can share tips with other sellers in similar markets, explore new suppliers and product lines, and learn about trending developments in your industry.

If you sell any type of job coaching, resume, or interview services, I would work on building contacts, joining groups, and positioning myself as an expert.

If you sell high end products—audio, consumer electronics, and gourmet foods work on building contacts. Post pictures, videos, and articles that position you as an expert in your industry. Join like-minded groups, answer questions in forums and communities, and work on optimizing your profile so people can find you.

Whatever you do—don't sell.

LinkedIn is a community of professionals. Other members will tune you out at the slightest indication you're trying to make a sale. Instead concentrate on sharing top quality information people will use, like, and appreciate. If you do this on a consistent basis the right people will find you.

LinkedIn 101

The trick to being found on LinkedIn is to fill out your profile as completely as possible.

Before you do that, however, you need to determine what you want to accomplish on LinkedIn. Do you want to get leads for the products you sell? Do you want to connect with leaders in your industry? Or do you just want to move as much product as possible?

There are no wrong answers.

Just understand your goals determine how you're going to approach LinkedIn.

The first thing you need to do is set up a well-optimized profile. It all starts with a professional photograph. If the prospects you want to attract wear a suit and tie, then you need a headshot showing you in a suit and tie. If your target audience is more casual, a polo or button up shirt will do. For women, you can never go wrong in a dress or pantsuit. Tone the makeup down, and steer clear of flashy colors.

Next on the list is your headline. You've got 120 characters to make it work, so get down to brass tacks.

To get your headline right, you've got to think like the people you want to attract. What keywords are they likely to use to find you? Is your location important? Should you include some of the key products you sell? This is important because LinkedIn is going to use these keywords to display your profile in search. If you use the wrong keywords you're going to be off the radar for over 90 percent of LinkedIn users.

LinkedIn has a new feature open to all users—a cover photo. It gives you one more chance to wow people who view your profile. Make sure it conveys what you're about. If you're an author your cover photo should show the covers of your most relevant books. If you're selling something it should show your key products being used by real people. If services are your game—list the services you offer in large letters. Show the benefits in a series of bullet points. If possible include a tagline, "Cover letters geared towards fortune 500 executives." "Gourmet drinks so good they're sinfully delicious."

The optimal size for your cover photo is 1400 x 425 pixels. And, here's one more tip. Don't make your own cover photo; hire a professional designer on Fiverr or elance. It's too important to leave anything to chance.

If you get these three things right you're ahead of ninety percent of the users on LinkedIn. Remember—Profile photo, headline, and cover photo.

Next up is your summary.

This is where you tell your story. You've got 2,000 characters to tell visitors what you're all about, why they should deal with you, and why you're the right guy to solve their problem.

I'm an ecommerce writer so I lead with my value statement. "Short easy to read solutions for your ecommerce problems." That sets the tone for everything else I have to say. It's a promise I make to readers, and everything I say from this point on needs to make good on that promise and reinforce it.

Your summary should tell people what you're all about. It's your value statement.

Brag a little bit.

Use this space to breathe a little life into your profile. Talk about what drives you. Your passions, your favorite sport teams, or a local charity you're active in. Or if you're all business: talk about your business. How'd you get into this line of work? What do you like about it? What value do you bring to the table for new customers?

After your summary comes work experience.

This is your traditional resume. For online sellers this may or may not be relevant. If your past work experience ties in with the products you sell go ahead and include it. If it's not relevant or you prefer not to share your work history you can leave this section blank. Just include your online business.

You can add value to your eBay business by collecting recommendations and endorsements from your customers and vendors. If you can collect five to ten recommendations for your eBay business it's going to make you stand out head-and-shoulders over your competition. No one else is doing this.

Another section highlights your volunteer experience. I'd recommend everyone take some time to fill this out. Volunteer experience is a great way to connect with like-minded individuals. It's going to humanize you in a way work experience won't. Let's go back to the example of our sports card seller. If he lists experience coaching a Dad's Club soccer team or a Little League baseball team it's going to position him as someone with a true passion for sports. If you sell Girl Scout supplies on eBay, other moms are going to look at you differently when you mention you spent ten years leading Brownie and Girl Scout troops.

Publications and Projects offer two more ways to position yourself as an expert in your field. Highlight any publications you contributed to, even if it's just a Xeroxed booklet you hand out to clients. It shows you know your stuff, and people value your experience. Projects are a way to highlight your organizational and management skills. The key to describing any projects or publications you've participated in is to slant them towards your online business.

How to Use LinkedIn

LinkedIn recently started letting users post content to the site—pictures, videos, and written content. This is an amazing opportunity to stand out and grow your authority.

My suggestion is to make short written posts of 350 to 750 words once or twice a week. If you can do it, post a 1500 to 2500 word article once a month. The easiest way to do this is to just start writing. Don't worry that you're not a writer. What you say doesn't have to be fancy. Oftentimes the best content is special, just because it contains the information people want and need.

If you're at a loss for ideas, think about trending topics in your niche, new products that are about to be released, and the everyday questions buyers ask you. Answer one or two questions in every post, and stick with it. Over time readers will come back week after week to find out what's next.

Success won't happen overnight. But if you're in it for the long haul, and post consistently you will build a following, and many of your readers will eventually check out the links to your eBay and Amazon stores.

Every so often you should shake things up.

Post a relevant photo or video. Include a short description telling viewers why it's important. Curiosity will entice people to take a peek.

Keep in mind, when you first get started the only people who are going to see your posts are your contacts. As time goes on, and they share your content with their followers your network will grow, and more people will be aware of what you're doing.

Another way to connect with people on LinkedIn is to join groups.

Groups are simply congregations of like-minded individuals who post questions and discussions in a private area on LinkedIn. Members are free to comment and join in the conversation. One thing I'd suggest is to spend a few days checking out different groups and learning how the members interact. Whatever you do, don't just jump in and start commenting before you understand the dynamics of the groups. Other members can check out your profile if they want to learn more about you, instead concentrate on providing quality information.

More than any other social medial network LinkedIn is going to require you to be in it for the long haul. If you stick with it, and keep interacting with other members you will grow a strong network that c can help you grow your sales.

Interviews

The previous section covered the nuts and bolts of social media marketing. What it is, an introduction to the various social media sites, and a brief overview of how to use them.

The problem is that leaves a big knowledge gap because all you have to go on is what I said, so you're not sure if using social media is worth the time and effort you need to invest in it.

It also leaves you wondering, "Is the stuff this guy's telling me everything I need to know."

That's why I turned to the experts—the eBay and Amazon sellers who are currently using social media to ignite their businesses. These conversations with them tell you what did and didn't work, and which social media sites they felt worked best.

Listen to what they have to say. Use the tips and tricks they give you to grow your business even stronger.

Interview with Lauren Lerner

I recently conducted an interview with Lauren Lerner of **Lauren's Fab Finds.** *Lauren has been selling on eBay since 1999 and runs a high end women's fashion site on eBay. She is doing an amazing job of using email and social media marketing to power up her sales. The contents of this interview should prove enlightening to sellers who are struggling to grow their sales.*

You can view Lauren's Fab Finds on eBay by following this link. http://stores.ebay.com/Laurens-Fab-Finds

. . . .

You're doing most of the things I talk about in this book: email marketing, Facebook, Pinterest, and You Tube. My first question is, how much time do you spend daily managing your social media activities? I know a lot of sellers who are going to say, "Sure, I'd like to do that, but who has the time?"

We spend quite a bit of time on social media. One of our staff handles the majority of it. He schedules almost all of our posts for the week. Some of the posts are scheduled through Hoot Suite so we can have them ready to go when needed. Others are posted in real time. Then there is time spent going through social media and responding to other peoples posts - like fashion bloggers, shopping experts, etc.

. . . .

What would you say to sellers who insist "That's too much work, especially when I don't know if it's going to pay off or not."

If you want to see an ROI on your social media efforts you need to put the time into this, just like you would spend the time to do a print media campaign or a media buy on television. You have to spend time thinking about what is your goal with social media and how can you achieve your goal. For some people it's just about putting up funny or cute posts....for other people it is about brand awareness....and for others it's about driving traffic to your website.

. . . .

There are so many choices out there: Facebook, Pinterest, or YouTube. Which channel works best for you, or do they all complement each other?

They do all complement each other. We are careful not to put the same exact content up on all three. Some things that we do are specific to each platform and we include Instagram and Twitter along with the three you listed. Facebook, YouTube and Twitter are three that get us the most engagement with our customers. Since our core customer base is women between the ages of 35 - 60, we focus on Facebook because that demographic uses Facebook the most.

....

You have a nice looking YouTube channel packed full of videos. Video is scary for a lot of folks, especially getting started. What would you recommend for someone just getting started with video?

Don't be scared. It's not live television. You can practice and get good at it. With today's technology all you need is a phone and simple editing software and you are all set. Start small with short commercials and then work yourself up to bigger things. However, keep your branding. If you are a high end retailer, your videos need to have that same look. It can't look like a kid made the video.

....

What types of video work best for you?

We do informational videos and sales video all the time. They work really well for us. When we are about to start a new sale, we will promote it with a video. Since we are an online store, the videos give our customers a real connection to me and some of my staff. They can see us and have a sense of what we are like because of the videos.

....

Do you script everything out, or do you just start the camera rolling and go at it?

The videos are definitely scripted. I have a staff member who writes, directs and produces all the videos. These videos are all thought out and planned very well. If you just ad-lib it, you will find that you are wasting a lot of time and the finished product will not look as good.

. . . .

I know I just started doing a lot of video reviews on Amazon, and the hardest part was getting started. I finally bit the bullet, fired up the camera on my iPhone, and started talking. I'm pretty sure I'd still be stalled out at the start zone if I'd kept trying to plan everything out. Is "just doing it" the best way to get started?

I would suggest having someone shoot the videos for you. If you want to practice your videos on your own, that is fine. But when it comes time to shoot the real thing, you want someone else to do it. Again, we are a high end fashion store, and our videos need to have that kind of feel to it. I can't do that by myself.

. . . .

I really like the cover page for your YouTube Channel. It's a perfect extension of your brand. Is that necessary to increasing your reach, or is it something that can wait until you grow your stock of videos?

This is all about branding. And our cover page is a part of it. When people come to our YouTube channel they know where they have landed. There is no reason to wait to put up the cover page. If you were a brick and mortar store, you would make sure your storefront sign was up before you had your grand opening.

....

I know from my own experience writing and marketing books, email is where it's at. Does email marketing drive your eBay sales? By that I mean, if you add a new product to your lineup, or run a sale with Mark Down Manager, do you find email marketing is an effective way to make more sales?

The eBay marketing newsletter really doesn't do well for us because there is no customization. We use Mail Chimp, and it helps remind our customers about sales and promotions. We rely on email marketing heavily to keep our name in front of our customers.

....

eBay is very protective of its customers, and takes a dim view of sellers contacting them to make off eBay sales. With that in mind, could you tell me a little about how you built your email list, and drove customers to your Facebook and Pinterest pages?

We build our list a few ways. First, there is a sign up form on our website. Second, every time we ship a package to a customer who bought something from our eBay store we include a professionally designed flyer. There is a QR code on the flyer that takes customers directly to our sign up form. Also, through all our social media campaigns, when someone engages with us on Facebook, Twitter, Instagram or Pinterest there are opportunities to sign up for the newsletter. There are also posts that we usually do once a week to promote signing up for our newsletters.

....

Let's say I'm a seller just starting out with email marketing. What kind of stuff do I send to my email list? Do I tell them about all of the great things I have for sale, or is it better to send them general information relating to the products I sell? I know with book marketing, we figure you should send one sales message for every ten information pieces. Are the rules the same for marketing your eBay business, or do you focus more on the items you have for sale?

With us, we focus 95% on sales. But we do that in different ways. The messages always vary. For example…

• *Why pay retail, shop Lauren's Fab Finds and save 50% - 85% off retail stores*

• *Don't miss out on our newest listings including…*

• *Promoting a specific sale….*

• *Promoting rare and hard to find items that we are about to list to the general public…*

• *Sometimes we do market fashion tips as well…*

....

eBay has a mailing list feature they use to send out regular emails to customers who subscribe to your list. If eBay is already contacting your customers, is it really necessary to do your own mailing?

And, I ask this for two reasons.

First, eBay's newsletters are pretty tacky. If you haven't seen them, it's probably because they're so forgettable. eBay's newsletters are just a group of links to some of the products you have for sale. They don't offer any information about your business, your brand, or what's going on in your niche.

Second, I don't know if you remember back in the day. Constant Contact provided an email newsletter service for eBay sellers. They sent a real newsletter to customers with articles that matched your customer's interests. What I liked was they tracked sales generated by their newsletters, and told you how many sales resulted from each issue. That way, there were no doubts whether email marketing worked, or not.

Do you find that your email newsletters tend to increase your sales?

We do use the eBay mail feature but get very limited, if any results. We use Mail Chimp for our newsletter because of the customization and list acquisition features.

....

There are laws that prohibit marketers from just putting customer names on your email list. That's why it's important to use a service like Mail Chimp or AWeber, because they take care of the legalities involved in opting customers in and out of your list.

With that in mind, what things did you do to get customers to join your mail list?

I mentioned how we acquire customers for our mailing list above. I do agree with you about the legalities. And that is one of the reasons that we use Mail Chimp.

....

Sellers have so many choices to promote their business these days: social media, email, and video. Do you think it's important to include social media in your eBay business, or is it just something to experiment with if you have some spare time?

I think social media, email and video are essential tools to grow your business. I wouldn't experiment with them.

I would make them a key part of your marketing strategy.

. . . .

Let's go back to email marketing. I know it's hard to put a dollar figure on your ROI from any kind of advertising, but after you've done it for a while, are you able to gage the effect a particular email campaign will have? Or is it more like sprinkling fairy dust, you put some out there and hope it will sprout wings and fly?

It is definitely not like fairy dust.

But that's not to say every email campaign gets a good ROI. Email marketing is a very inexpensive way to remind your customers about your sales, promotions or any other information that is relevant. Whether you use Mail Chimp, Constant Contact or any other email service, the cost is going to be a few hundred dollars at most.

If you are just starting out, and don't have a very large database, there are even free services. It's mostly your time that is biggest "expense."

We plan out our email campaigns every 3 months and adjust accordingly based on how sales are going and if we have any last minute promotions. We track data for every one of our email campaigns. I know how many people opened the email, which specific links were clicked and which forms were filled out. If there is an offer to buy something, I can also track how many sales were generated from the campaign.

. . . .

Most eBay sellers have no idea what email marketing is about let alone how to get started. What types of emails would you suggest they send out for their first campaigns? I know you say you have a sales goal or message you try to spread for most of your mailings.

How important is it for sellers new to email to plan their email campaigns before shooting them out to customer's email boxes?

For a first campaign you could do a "Sign Up for our Newsletter and Receive a Discount." Refer a Friend and Save." Or you could do something where you give good information to your customers. For us it could be "Top 10 Spring Fashions."

It is crucial to have plan for email marketing.

You don't want to do it too much or too little. And you also want your emails to complement your other marketing strategies like social media post, etc. Everything should be planned out to complement each other.

. . . .

Let's say my time is limited and I only have time to post on one or two social media sites? How do I decide which ones will give me the biggest bang for my buck, or for the time I invest.

Great question! It really depends on your audience, so you need to do some market research. Our customers are mainly women between the ages of 35 - 55. They are primarily on Facebook, and that is why we focus on them. If we were selling to teenagers, we would focus more on Instagram. So you can't really paint a broad brush and say that Facebook should be everyone's first priority. We go Facebook first, and Twitter second.

. . . .

All of your marketing communications have the same basic look and feel to them. When I visit your website, eBay store, Pinterest or Facebook page, I recognize right off that they are part of Lauren's Fab Finds. How important is it that sellers retain that consistent look and feel in everything they do?

Branding is extremely important for any company. We want a client to see us on any platform and know they are looking at Lauren's Fab Finds. Think about a major retailer like Coke. Their image is the same whether it is on TV, Billboards, Print Ads, Internet, etc. The same goes for an eBay business.

. . . .

Let's say I only have time for one social media platform. Which one would you suggest? Email marketing – Facebook – Pinterest – Instagram – YouTube?

If it was only one it would be Email Marketing.

Grow your list and send relevant information to your subscribers. On social media, you never know if it is being seen. With email marketing at least you know it is being delivered. If you consistently send your subscribers timely and relevant information, your emails will have a good open rate.

. . . .

Last year eBay released their own spin on social media – collections, followers, etc. What is your take on them? Are they important to sellers, or just another time suck sellers should steer clear of?

It is not really relevant to us. We list items that our customers want at prices they want to pay. That is what is going to make them come back and be repeat buyers. It is a nice feature that eBay offers but we don't spend time on it.

....

Store owners have the ability to discount select items using Mark Down Manager, and the Promotions Manager that allows them to issue coupons, offer free shipping, or provide discounts for multiple purchases. What's your take on these tools? How have they worked for you?

These are ok for us. We use them, but don't rely on them too heavily. Again, I will go back to email marketing. If I use the Mark Down Manager to try to generate sales, and at the same time do an email marketing campaign, the ROI on the email campaign will be about 10X higher.

....

Is there anything else you think readers should know?

Don't look at your business as "just an eBay business". Think of your business as an online retailer. Your advertising and marketing efforts need to be relevant to your customers, with the same branding and you have to use multiple platforms.

Interview with Cameron Loughlin

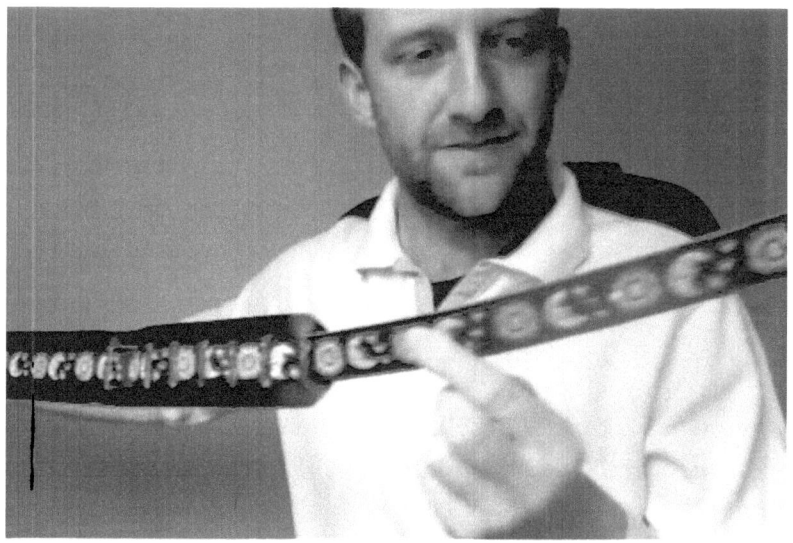

I recently conducted an interview with Cameron Loughlin, owner of Tempest Leather. He markets custom guitar straps (guaranteed for life) on his own website and on Amazon, and has been an eBay seller in a past life. Cameron has some good tips on using social media marketing that eBay sellers should find relevant.

You're doing most of the things I talk about in this book: email marketing, Facebook, Pinterest, and You Tube. My first question is, how much time do you spend daily managing your social media activities? I know a lot of sellers who are going to say, "Sure, I'd like to do that, but who has the time?"

I only spend about half an hour a day managing social media and most of is it is spent on Facebook. Facebook allows me to schedule posts ahead of time, so I'll spend a Saturday morning planning a sale for Monday and then I'll fine tune it on Sunday.

Consistency is the key to standing out in the minds of your customers. Update it as much as you realistically can, but remember that **it's a long game** *and ultimately it's better to have longevity and post a little then to post all the time and burn out after a year. I think a ton of businesses burn out because they aren't willing to stick with it over many years. My suggestion is to carve out an hour a week to start and just start posting pictures, articles and even giveaways if you have a product/service ready to go.*

. . . .

What would you say to sellers who insist "That's too much work, especially when I don't know if it's going to pay off, or not."

I would tell them to remember that most successful businesses win with the marathon approach not the sprint.

If you do a little every week, and sustain it for years you'll develop trust with you customers and you'll make new ones through word of mouth. The key is constantly getting better and knowing that it won't all happen at once. Hard work tends to be rewarded over time, but you have to love what you do to stick with it. Also, I would tell them that any kind of positive results from a social media campaign early on can really inspire because you it fires you up to keep going.

. . . .

There are so many choices out there: Facebook, Pinterest, or YouTube. Which channel works best for you, or do they all complement each other?

Facebook is the best by far for me.

It's simply the most interactive and fun. People are constantly logged into Facebook, and they are reading their newsfeed all the time. It's so easy to take a picture of your product or service and then put together a post. I actually have my Facebook account linked to my Twitter account so my updates occur simultaneously on both platforms. In this sense they complement each other well. **Side note***: Running Facebook ads can get you many "likes" but might not get you an immediate ROI, so you need to think about it how it fits into your budget at first.*

. . . .

You mention that you have a YouTube channel. Video is scary for a lot of folks, especially getting started. What would you recommend for someone just getting started with video?

Great question. Create something of high value that your customers need.

1.   What is the question that your customers are asking themselves when they buy your product or service?
2.   How can you help them?

In our case I created a video on how to assemble a guitar strap, and now it almost has 1,000 views. Put yourself in the customers' shoes and go from there. What is frustrating to your customer, and how can you solve their problem?

. . . .

Do you script everything out, or do you just start the camera rolling and go at it?

I will write down bullet points that I refer to. I do multiple takes and then I take breaks and get back at it later in the day. I find that my speaking ability improves over the course of the day, and I become clearer on the topic.

. . . .

I know I just started doing a lot of video reviews on Amazon, and the hardest part for me was getting started. I finally bit the bullet, fired up the camera on my iPhone, and started talking. I'm pretty sure I'd still be stalled out at the start zone if I'd kept trying to plan everything out. Is "just doing it" the best way to get started?

Yes, and don't underestimate the power of having small success early on and just getting *something* out there. Any kind of positive reaction or sale will help you keep going. It's amazing how fired up I got over even one sale in the beginning.

Try to get it out quickly, because then you can get feedback and learn how to improve before you develop a full product or service line. The quicker you can fire up the iPhone or iMac camera to make a video the better.

. . . .

eBay is very protective of its customers. They take a dim view of sellers contacting customers to make off eBay sales. With that in mind, could you tell me a little about how you built your email list, and drove customers to your Facebook and Pinterest pages?

I would recommend using online giveaway software such as gleam.io to collect email addresses. This is a great way to ethically market to people. You can utilize this software through Facebook.

. . . .

Let's go back to Pinterest. It's such a visual site. I know I have several boards there. I pinned pictures of my books and blog posts and they get repined every day.

What's your experience with Pinterest? What type of stuff works best for you, and more importantly are you seeing results from it?

Pinterest is a nice passive platform for our company. I looked on Pinterest the other day and noticed my product was pinned many times, and I never did anything to promote it on Pinterest. But people saw my website, my Etsy site, and Amazon products, and then they pinned pictures of our guitar straps to Pinterest.

Pinterest is a nice platform in this sense but I haven't invested much time and energy into it directly. I'm glad it's there because it helps drive traffic to our site when people see our pins!

. . . .

How important is it that sellers retain that consistent look and feel in everything they do? Should all of your social media sites, your website, and eBay store have the same look and feel to them?

Consistent branding is an important characteristic that ties your message together. When you're very consistent it clarifies the message you're sending out. There are millions of marketing messages going out every week and by having a concise, uniform message you can get people's attention.

....

Let's say I only have time for one social media platform. Which one would you suggest? Email marketing – Facebook – Pinterest – Instagram – YouTube?

Facebook—all the way. It's more dynamic than the other platforms, and a great way to interact with your customers. It's very easy to run advertisements to drive impressions, clicks, and even sales.

....

Is there anything else you think readers should know?

I think the key is sticking with whatever you do from a marketing standpoint. Occasionally a business will see a post go viral and blow up, but most of the time it's a slow process that takes a while.

Don't give up and do a little every day!

Interview with Carla Z

Carla Z believes in the magic of ordinary days. All of her business endeavors reflect that quality.

Carla is the proprietor of the eBay store Vintage Value PA, a business she began in January 2015. Told for years she has a good eye towards vintage finds, antiques, collectibles and unusual objects d'art, she decided to take the plunge and form an Internet-based business. A purveyor of smaller vintage and unusual treasures, her motto is "My pick is your gain! Treat yourself to a treasure!"

www.ebay.com/usr/vintagevaluepa is her eBay page.

https://www.facebook.com/VintageValuePA is the Facebook page for her business.

https://www.pinterest.com/pinupgirlpa is her Pinterest page.

You're doing several of the things I talk about in this book: Pinterest and Facebook. My first question is how much time do you spend daily managing your social media activities? I know a lot of sellers who are going to say, "Sure, I'd like to do that, but who has the time?"

It just depends on the day and what time I actually have to do it. Sometimes it's half an hour sometimes it's a couple of hours.

. . . .

What would you say to sellers who insist "That's too much work, especially when I don't know if it's going to pay off or not?"

It's not so much work it's just getting into a routine. It's easy. And it's free publicity and advertising so what is so bad about that?

. . . .

Pinterest is one of those sites that intrigues me most. It's very visual, and easy to use. It's also the site sellers tell me is most effective. What is your experience with Pinterest?

Pinterest is literally a giant pin board.

It's great for ideas and saving recipes and posting things you like. People go there looking for inspiration, and even collectibles they are hunting for.

I don't know for certain if any of my eBay sales have been a result of Pinterest, but I can tell you when I post on Pinterest I get a lot more hits on my listings.

. . . .

What type of items do you post on Pinterest? Do you just post the items you have for sale, or do you mix them with videos, product reviews, pictures, and other content?

I post on Pinterest for household ideas, decorating ideas, beautiful high-end couture fashion, my eBay items, recipes, gardening tips. I am also a photographer so sometimes I post some of my photos.

I get ideas for holiday decorating and things like that. It is also a terrific resource if you are a crafter.

. . . .

A lot of social media *gurus* suggest you write a keyword driven description for each item you pin. What do you think of that?

Truthfully there are only so many hashtags I can stand in a day.

I don't hashtag my items.

I might hashtag on Twitter, but that has nothing to do with anything I'm selling on eBay or pinning on Pinterest.

. . . .

Last question, is social media worth it? Is it essential to making your business a success, or just one more thing to do?

Social media is a blessing and a curse.

As someone who has been a blogger for years I've discovered it works both ways (I.e. a blessing and a curse).

You have to learn how to handle your social media properly, but I do believe it is beneficial to businesses depending upon how you do it.

Some people think they have to hire someone to do their social media, and that's fine but you better make sure they know your business and your voice and your customer base before they begin. I have seen businesses get into a pickle with customers because they had some person who really didn't know their business doing their social media and the customers caught on and not in a positive way.

I learned how to use social media first as a community activist. I was part of a group fighting eminent domain for private gain in the days of Kelo vs. New London. As part the grassroots group we didn't have the money for advertising or marketing or anyone to do it for us, so we learned.

It wasn't so hard, and it's fun.

Social media is a valuable tool. *And I think learning to do your own social media effectively keeps you connected and fresh with your business.*

. . . .

Can we talk about Facebook for a minute?

I see a lot of sellers who post every one of their listings on their Facebook page. It's a crazy strategy because it's got to drive your followers away, especially if you post fifty, one hundred, or more items a week. Can you say un-friend.

Now that I said that, what types of content do you feel eBay sellers should post on Facebook?

I have a dedicated and separate page on Facebook for my business.

Once in a while if I think I have something that will appeal to my personal Facebook friends I will share a listing on my personal page, but I don't post all of my listings.

I will post articles about what I sell, and other related things like pins I have found on Pinterest that inspire me. I will also share items I have found that interest me on like-minded Facebook pages.

I'm totally with you on the annoying factor because there is a woman on my Facebook page that I am friendly with who runs several Facebook yard sale type groups. She is always hunting an angle and it annoys me no end. But fortunately the beautiful thing about Facebook is you can still like a page or be friends with someone but not follow them if you follow me.

I am a vintage/collectibles/smalls seller and most of my things are for the home and at price points that won't break the bank, so if I see an article about repurposing or decorating or what is hot now in the world of collectibles I will post that, because if it interests me it'll interest others.

Some things I post on Facebook, some on Pinterest, but not every single thing I am selling.

I figure if people check out one of my items via Facebook or Pinterest they are intelligent enough to see what else I am listing for sale. I am new to all of this relatively speaking but my approach is simple: I sell things that I would like to buy for myself, and I sort of stick to that rule of thumb when I am posting – what would I like to see?

....

Probably the hardest thing about Facebook, is getting people your page, and then getting them to like things once they are there. How do you direct your customers to your Facebook or Pinterest pages? Do you just hope they find you? Do you include links with every item you mail out, or is there some other trick to it?

I do not include links to my pages when I mail out items. And the thing about Facebook and Pinterest is it just takes time. I tell my customers they can find me on Facebook and Pinterest if they ask. I prefer not to inundate people.

Once a while I will share my business Facebook page on my personal page and ask people if they have liked that. Every time I do that I get a few more likes, and people they know like it in turn.

When you are setting up a Facebook page for your business they now sort of give you a place where you can basically tag the categories you fall into so that also helps attract new people.

I will also comment on things compatible with my business, and that draws people to my page. When I am putting other people's pins on Pinterest, it also draws people to my Pinterest items that way. And I will like similar business pages as my business on Facebook.

Even in a virtual Internet setting, there is still that old-fashioned thing called networking.

Interview with Heather Peterson

Heather Peterson's Amazon store is called Girl Charlee. She offers fabrics and sewing products to followers there and from her own website https://girlcharlee.com/. In this interview she shares some information with us on how she uses Pinterest to drive her online sales.

How much time do you spend daily managing your social media activities? I know a lot of sellers who are going to say, "Sure, I'd like to do that, but who has the time?"

We spend about 3 hours a day managing our different social media activities as well as social media member groups.

. . . .

What would you say to sellers who insist "That's too much work, especially when I don't know if it's going to pay off or not?"

I would say you are missing out on a great way to grow your brand and generate revenue!

By getting your brand and products consistently in front of a wide range of potential customers you are able to boost sales and product awareness.

By mixing in a personal engaging touch people relate to your company on a more personal level that in turn promotes brand and product loyalty and drives increased sales.

. . . .

Pinterest is one of the social media site that intrigues me most. It's very visual, and easy to use. It's also the site sellers tell me is most effective. What is your experience with Pinterest?

Pinterest is very effective for marketing. It allows you to create different areas of visual interest for pinners that ultimately drives traffic back to your storefront and create sales.

. . . .

What type of items do you post on Pinterest? Do you just post the items you have for sale, or do you mix them with videos, product reviews, pictures, and other content?

We sell fabric so we can pin our new arrival fabrics, but we also re-pin sewing tutorials, sewing patterns, and other related interesting collateral that allows pinners to re-pin the content to their boards with our name and logo on it which in turn drives traffic back to us.

. . . .

A lot of social media *gurus* suggest you write a keyword driven description for each item you pin. What do you think of that?

Agreed! You have to have content rich information in the pin description. That way if someone is searching for that particular keyword your pin will be presented in the results.

. . . .

Pinterest has a feature where you can add the price to your pins if it's an item you have for sale. Do you use that feature, and if you do--how effective is it?

Yes, Rich Pins are a must! For our product pins we feed Pinterest the product name, website URL, price, and keyword rich description. This allows the pinner to see as much information as possible to entice them to click through for purchase. This information also persists with all re-pins.

. . . .

What about setting up your profile, and your Pinterest About section (or bio)? You get 160 characters to tell viewers all about you. That's not a lot of space. What type of stuff should sellers include in their Pinterest bio?

Convert your Pinterest account into a business account and use your logo and tagline and URL to match your branding and marketing. Never waste an opportunity to get your name and brand out there!

....

Last question, is social media worth it? Is it essential to making your business a success, or just one more thing to do?

For any business, especially online businesses, social media is a must!

In order to get your brand and products in front of potentially millions of people each day there is no better alternative. When used in conjunction with an internet marketing strategy it is the best way to grow a business successfully.

Bonus Excerpt

(Here's an excerpt from one of my newest books, **eBay Bookkeeping Made Easy***. This section focuses on how to use GoDaddy Bookkeeping to track your sales, expenses, and profits. You can check the entire book out by following this link, eBay Bookkeeping Made Easy.)*

Getting started with GoDaddy Bookkeeping

GoDaddy Bookkeeping is available as an app you can download from eBay's applications bar. Amazon and Etsy sellers can check out the online version by visiting this link http://www.godaddy.com/accounting/accounting-software.aspx?isc=gooob012&ci=87249.

The service was originally known as Outright, and was taken over by GoDaddy last year. It's an online accounting solution that will serve the needs of most users. It automatically imports transaction data from your PayPal account, and posts it to the proper categories. Users can also synch their business credit cards and checking accounts with the service.

For sellers conducting business on multiple platforms GoDaddy Bookkeeping can import transaction data from eBay, Amazon and Etsy. It also works with several invoicing services including FreshBooks, Shoeboxed, and Harvest.

Here's the least you need to know. GoDaddy Bookkeeping is available in the *Applications* tab on your *My eBay* page. Hover your mouse over *Applications* until it shows Manage Applications, click on this and scroll through the list of applications until you come to *Outright*. Click on *Outright*, and select *Try it Free*.

GoDaddy Bookkeeping is available as a monthly ($9.99) or yearly ($99.00) subscription. Choose your poison and follow the prompts to get started.

Overview

The first page you see is your account overview. It contains all of the basic information about your account. In the upper right corner it shows your yearly profit or loss so you can tell at a glance where you stand. Below this is a graph that charts your income and expenses, a pie chart that shows your current month's expenses, and then a list of open invoices.

Below this is a section that shows Invoice Activity. Most online sellers aren't going to use this feature as all of your invoicing is done through eBay, Amazon, Etsy, and your ecommerce storefronts. If you're running a side business where your customers pay through PayPal this is where you would bill your customers for products or services sold.

In the left hand column you'll see four small blue boxes. The first box is labeled *New This Week* and tracks your new sales, and any uncategorized expenses. To view your new transactions or uncategorized expenses click on the number, and it will take you to your general ledger.

The *Money I Have Box* lets you view the balances in your accounts – PayPal, Amazon, and any bank accounts you have connected.

The Money I Owe box shows your liabilities or the money you owe. Some of the accounts shown here are your eBay balance, and money owed to Amazon and Etsy for seller fees.

The last box is labeled *Taxes*. It shows you several key tax indicators for your business. The first line shows your estimated quarterly tax payment, and when it is due. The mileage line shows your year to date mileage expenses. When you click on mileage it takes you to your general ledger and lets you log your mileage. The last line shows your *Sales Tax Liability*, so you always know how much you owe.

Below the four blue boxes you should see two blue bars. *Add Account* lets you add your various seller accounts, PayPal Account, and any bank accounts you want to tie into GoDaddy Bookkeeping. *Refresh All* imports data from your connected accounts so that you're viewing the most recent information available.

If you scroll back up to the top of the page you'll see your six control tabs – Overview, Income, Expenses, Reports, Taxes, and Manage. When you click on any of these they open more program options.

Before I describe the control tabs there's one other item I should cover. Sometimes a tan bar will appear just below the control tab. It shows program alerts or problems GoDaddy Bookkeeping may be experiencing with your account. When you click on the Fix It highlight it will walk you through solving the problem so you can get your program up and running correctly again.

....

You can view your profit & loss statement anytime by clicking on the *view details* tab underneath where it says *(Year) Profit & Loss* on the GoDaddy Bookkeeping *Overview* page.

Your Profit & Loss statement gives you a quick overview of the financial health of your business. The top section shows your sources of income, and the bottom section details your expenses. The final line shows your "bottom line," or the actual profit or loss your business is making.

The default view for your P & L is the previous twelve months, but you have the option to change that any time you'd like. Scroll up to the top of the page under *Profit & Loss* where you see *ending*. You can choose the ending month or year, or you can change the time period to day, week, month, quarter, or year. To return to the chart select the chart icon on the right hand side.

If you want to take a closer look at a transaction all of the items on your P & L are clickable. Select the one you want to examine and it will take you to the general ledger page for that category.

Moving back down to the bottom of the page you will see two tabs at the far right side. Export lets you transfer P & L information to a Microsoft Excel file. Selecting print will give you a hard copy of your P & L.

Income

The income tab lets you manage your online income accounts. When you click on income it takes you to your general ledger page for income, and you can view your most recent transactions.

Once again, all of the transactions displayed are clickable. If you want to edit a transaction select it, and make the needed corrections.

What I recommend here is to set up categories for all of your income transactions so you can track where your money is coming from. When GoDaddy Bookkeeping imports income transactions it brings all of them in under the general "sales" heading. If you're just selling on one venue, such as eBay or Amazon, that's not a problem. If you sell across multiple platforms it's important to know the source your money is coming from. This way you can take corrective action if a sales venue is underperforming.

The first thing you need to know is every time you make a sale GoDaddy Bookkeeping records it as two separate transactions. The merchandise portion is recorded under the "sales" heading. If postage was charged on the transaction it is recorded under the heading "shipping income."

If you want to add additional sales categories select a transaction, and then scroll down the page until you see a heading labeled *Good to Know*. Over to the right hand side you will see a link labeled *Manage Categories*. Select it. This shows you a chart of your current income categories. To add a category select *New income Category*. Categorize it as *Business* or *Nonbusiness*, and then name the new category. After doing this you need to select a tax category. To tie the category you created to sales you would choose *gross receipts or sales*. Select *create*, and your new category is ready to use.

To give you an idea about how to use this, I added the following categories to my income account – eBay sales, Amazon, Bonanaza, *eBid*, bidStart, Kindle, Create Space, and Audible. By doing this I can keep separate tabs on each of my sales channels. It gives me better control over my business, and allows me to spot patterns early as they're beginning to emerge.

After you set up your income categories you need to assign each individual transaction to the proper category. The easiest way to do this is from the Overview page. Select *view details* to see your P & L. Click on *sales* in the income section of your P & L. This will pull up all of your unassigned items. Select each item separately, and assign it to the proper income account. This step is pretty straightforward and should take just a few moments a day.

Whenever you're working on your P & L you also want to take a look at your uncategorized expenses. They're listed at the bottom of the P & L, just before you see your bottom line. Most items are categorized when they're imported, but there are usually a few uncategorized items, either because you purchased from a new supplier and GoDaddy Bookkeeping doesn't know how to classify it, or because the items you purchased from that supplier may fit into several different expense categories. Click on the individual unclassified transactions and assign them to the proper category.

If you do this every time you open your program it will only take a few minutes of your time, and it will ensure your P & L is up-to-date and accurate.

Expenses

When you select expenses it brings up the general ledger view for your business expenses.

Similar to the income category you can set up personalized categories to customize GoDaddy Bookkeeping for your business needs. Select an individual expense to enter the edit mode. Scroll down the page until you see the heading *Good to Know*. Move your mouse to the far right of the page and click on *manage categories*. Select *new expense category* and follow the prompts. Categorize the expense as a business or nonbusiness expense and name it. Scroll through the *tax category list* to tie your new expense to the proper category, and then select *Create*.

I would suggest setting up custom categories for your internet and cell phone providers, storage space rental, etc.

I find it useful to lump a few expense categories together. The main category I do this with is postage. I throw all of my shipping expenses in there – boxes, packing tape, stay free mailers, peanuts, you name it. The reason I do this is it makes it easier to compare my shipping expenses and shipping income. As long as the shipping income is equal to or more than my shipping expense, I know I'm on the right track. When they get out of whack it's time for an intervention to determine what went wrong.

With my other expenses my main concern is that they're consistent from month-to-month. If one month is way up without a similar bump in sales it's time to investigate what happened. Sometime it's a special purchase I had the opportunity to make; sometimes a number was entered wrong. The key thing is to watch your numbers and react quickly when you see that something is out of whack.

Reports

When you select reports it brings you to your Profit and loss statement. GoDaddy bookkeeping always shows you the chart first. Select *view as table* to see your P & L Statement.

If you're running a business you should know these numbers forwards and backwards. Growth is good, but I like to see consistent numbers across the board.

When I'm comparing my book sales numbers, the first thing I do is compare them with the last few months. If sales seem unusually low I take a peek at last year's numbers to see if it's a seasonal trend. You should do the same thing.

Online sales are always slower in summer. They normally pick up by late August and run strong through spring. February is a little iffy – it can go either way. The first half of November can be the same way waiting for Christmas buying to kick in.

Key point: Use your P & L to help forecast fluctuations in your business. Study it for trends, where sales are increasing or decreasing, or where expenses are rising. Put on your detective hat and figure out what's happening. Doing this will make you a better business person, and help your business to grow stronger over the long haul.

Taxes

The taxes section helps you with three specific areas.

1) It provides your Schedule C information to make tax time a breeze. Just transfer over the numbers and you're ready to file. Keep in mind you're still going to need a tax advisor or a good tax program like TurboTax Business or HR Block Business. GoDaddy Bookkeeping doesn't figure the home office deduction, tax credits, etc. They just provide you with the raw numbers to fill out your Schedule C.

2) GoDaddy tracks your sales taxes due, so it's easy to file and submit your state reports. As long as you have eBay, Amazon, and Etsy set up to collect sales tax in your state, GoDaddy Bookkeeping will track all of the information for you.

3) Every time you log into your account you are able to see your estimated tax payments and the date they are due. This way the due date and the amount you owe won't sneak up on you.

Manage

When you select manage it displays a list of all the accounts you have connected to GoDaddy Bookkeeping. If any of the accounts have errors you will see a tan bar displayed by them. Click on the blue *Fix It* link to take care of account issues.

If you want to connect more accounts, select *Add an Account* at the top of the page

. . . .

Good to know

You can easily reassign categories if something appears is mis-categorized.

Most often when this happens it's because the program does not recognize how to classify the transaction. To fix the problem select the item that needs to be classified. At the far right it will say uncategorized item, select the correct category from the drop down box, and press save.

You will also need to re-categorize items when you make a non-business related purchase. GoDaddy Bookkeeping has a *personal expense* category you can assign the item to so it is removed from your business records. If you sell a personal item and receive payment for an item through your PayPal account you can reassign it to the *personal income* category.

Best advice

Keep a close eye on your accounting program. Update it every few days. It's easier to catch errors when just a few items are displayed. If you let it go too long, a large list of items to re-categorize can seem overwhelming.

Books by Nick Vulich

eBay 2014: Why You're Not Selling Anything on eBay, and What you Can Do About it

Freaking Idiots Guide to Selling on eBay: How Anyone Can Make $100 or More Everyday Selling on eBay

Sell it Online: How to Make Money Selling on eBay, Amazon, Fiverr, & Etsy

Audio Books by Nick Vulich

eBay 2014: Why Your Stuff Isn't Selling And What You Can Do About It

Freaking Idiots guide to Selling on eBay: How anyone can make $100 or more everyday selling on eBay